SACRED PLACES

A PILGRIMAGE *of* PROMISE

A CANTATA INSPIRED BY EARLY AMERICAN SONG

By Joseph M. Martin

Full orchestration by Brant Adams • Consort orchestration by Stan Pethel

(1)   This symbol indicates a track number on the StudioTrax CD (accompaniment only) or SplitTrax CD.

Performance Time: ca. 45 Minutes

ISBN 9-781-4950-7877-4

EXCLUSIVELY DISTRIBUTED BY

7777 W. BLUEMOUND RD. P.O. BOX 13819 MILWAUKEE, WI 53213

Copyright © 2016 by HAL LEONARD - MILWIN MUSIC CORP.
International Copyright Secured   All Rights Reserved

In Australia Contact:
Hal Leonard Australia Pty. Ltd.
4 Lentara Court
Cheltenham, Victoria, 3192 Australia
Email: ausadmin@halleonard.com.au

For all works contained herein:
Unauthorized copying, arranging, adapting, recording, Internet posting, public performance,
or other distribution of the printed music in this publication is an infringement of copyright.
Infringers are liable under the law.

Visit Hal Leonard Online at
www.halleonard.com/church

Visit Shawnee Press Online at
www.shawneepress.com

FOREWORD

Sacred are the places that were witness to the life and works of the Savior. Holy is the ground where Jesus traveled during His ministry of grace. Divine are the windswept hills and the rolling plains, the valleys crisscrossed with rugged trails; those winding footpaths where the sandals of His followers kicked up the dust; eager pilgrims, hearts frenzied with faith, rejoicing in the new-breathed gospel.

In our hearts, let us walk together the ancient roads of Nazareth and pace along the golden shores of Galilee. Let us climb the rugged hills and trek the weathered stone streets. Let us take solace and refuge in the quiet gardens and rest beneath the olive trees. With pensive tread, let us walk the way of suffering and kneel in the shadow of Calvary's cross.

As we journey in our spirits to the sacred places of our shared faith, may we go in gratitude. May we travel with the expectation of encounter and the desire for discovery. May we walk the road in faith, with our eyes clearly fixed upon Jesus who meets us along the way. For He is our fellow traveler, our Shepherd, and our Guide. It is Christ who "is" the journey and the glorious journey's end. He alone is our divine destination, our pathway of promise, our sacred place.

SCRIPTURE FOR CONTEMPLATION

An angel appeared to Moses in the flames of a burning bush in the desert near Mount Sinai. When he saw this, he was amazed at the sight. As he went over to get a closer look, he heard the Lord say: "I am the God of your fathers, the God of Abraham, Isaac and Jacob." Moses trembled with fear and did not dare to look. Then the Lord said to him, "Take off your sandals, for the place where you are standing is holy ground." *Acts 7:30-33 (NIV)* *

PERFORMANCE NOTES

For Holy Week or Tenebrae services, it is recommended that the cantata end with "A Green Hill Far Away." The "Prelude" may then be played as a recessional.

For Easter or other celebratory services, the cantata should be performed in its entirety.

* THE HOLY BIBLE, NEW INTERNATIONAL VERSION®, NIV® Copyright © 1973, 1978, 1984, 2011 by Biblica, Inc.® Used by permission. All rights reserved worldwide.

PRELUDE

Tune: **RIDGECREST**
by JOSEPH M. MARTIN (BMI)

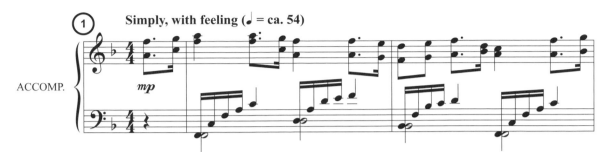

Copyright © 2002 by Malcolm Music, a div. of Shawnee Press, Inc.
This arrangement Copyright © 2016 by Malcolm Music, a div. of Shawnee Press, Inc.
International Copyright Secured   All Rights Reserved

Duplication of this publication is illegal, and duplication is not granted
by the CCLI, LicenSing or OneLicense.net licenses.

SACRED PLACES - SATB

4

THE RIVER JORDAN

Then Jesus came from Galilee to the Jordan to be baptized by John. But John tried to deter Him, saying, "I need to be baptized by You, and do You come to me?"

Jesus replied, "Let it be so now; it is proper for us to do this to fulfill all righteousness." Then John consented.

As soon as Jesus was baptized, He went up out of the water. At that moment heaven was opened, and He saw the Spirit of God descending like a dove and alighting on Him. And a voice from heaven said, "This is my Son, whom I love; with Him I am well pleased."

Matthew 3:13-17 (NIV) *

* THE HOLY BIBLE, NEW INTERNATIONAL VERSION®, NIV® Copyright © 1973, 1978, 1984, 2011 by Biblica, Inc.® Used by permission. All rights reserved worldwide.

SONGS FROM THE RIVER

Incorporating:
"As I Went Down in the River to Pray"
"The River Is Wide"
"Deep River"
"I've Got Peace Like a River"
Arranged by
JOSEPH M. MARTIN (BMI)

* Tune: RESTORATION, traditional American folk melody
** Tune: Traditional American folk melody
    Words: Traditional American folk song

Copyright © 2016 by HAL LEONARD - MILWIN MUSIC CORP.
International Copyright Secured   All Rights Reserved

Duplication of this publication is illegal, and duplication is not granted
by the CCLI, LicenSing or OneLicense.net licenses.

8

16

pray, stud-y-in' a-bout that good ol' way, and who shall

19

wear the robe and crown; good Lord, show me the way!

22 *a few sopranos***

mel.

Oh, sis-ters, let's go down._____ Let's go down.

25

Come on down. Oh, sis-ters, let's go down,

* Only a few sopranos should sing the top notes through m. 29
so that the melody is predominant.

SACRED PLACES - SATB

* Tune: O WALY, WALY, traditional folk melody
Words: Traditional folk song, alt.

SACRED PLACES - SATB

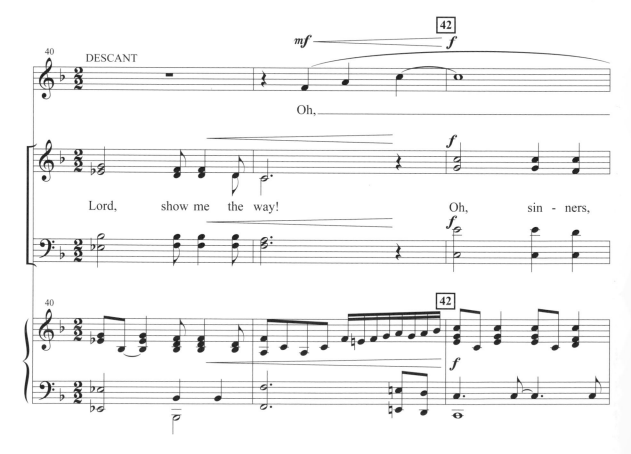

* Tune: DEEP RIVER, African-American spiritual
Words: African-American spiritual

SACRED PLACES - SATB

* Tune: PEACE LIKE A RIVER, African-American spiritual
Words: African-American spiritual

16

lost_____ but now I'm found.

I once was__ blind, but now I

I once was__ blind, but now I

see.

see. A - maz - ing

THE WEDDING AT CANA

On the third day (after Jesus' baptism) there was a wedding at Cana in Galilee, and the mother of Jesus was there. Jesus also was invited to the wedding with His disciples. When the wine ran out, the mother of Jesus said to Him, "They have no wine." And Jesus said to her, "Woman, what does this have to do with Me? My hour has not yet come." His mother said to the servants, "Do whatever He tells you."

Now there were six stone water jars there for the Jewish rites of purification, each holding twenty or thirty gallons. Jesus said to the servants, "Fill the jars with water." And they filled them up to the brim. And He said to them, "Now draw some out and take it to the master of the feast." So they took it. When the master of the feast tasted the water now become wine, and did not know where it came from (though the servants who had drawn the water knew), the master of the feast called the bridegroom and said to him, "Everyone serves the good wine first, and when people have drunk freely, then the poor wine. But you have kept the good wine until now." This, the first of His signs, Jesus did at Cana in Galilee, and manifested His glory. And His disciples believed in Him.

John 2:1-12 (adapted from ESV)*

* The ESV® Bible (The Holy Bible, English Standard Version®).
  Copyright © 2001 by Crossway, a publishing ministry of Good News Publishers.
  The ESV® text has been reproduced in cooperation with and by permission of Good News Publishers.
  Unauthorized reproduction of this publication is prohibited. All rights reserved.

COME AND HEAR THE WONDROUS STORY

Words by
JOSEPH M. MARTIN (BMI)

Tunes:
INVITATION
and **BEACH SPRING**
Arranged by
JOSEPH M. MARTIN

* Tune: INVITATION, traditional American folk melody

Copyright © 2016 by HAL LEONARD - MILWIN MUSIC CORP.
International Copyright Secured   All Rights Reserved

Duplication of this publication is illegal, and duplication is not granted
by the CCLI, LicenSing or OneLicense.net licenses.

SACRED PLACES - SATB

thirst for love di - vine.

mf unis.
Come, be - hold the____ King of

Come and____

glo - ry turn - ing wa - ter in - to____ wine.

bring your____ emp - ty spir - its. Bring your____ parched and____ wound - ed

souls. Lift your cups be - fore the Proph - et. He will

fill and make you whole.

Gath - er,

22

welcome. Let no__ one be__ turned a - way. Bro - ken

lives His____ heart em - brac - es. Mir - a - cles be - gin to -

day.

24 9

* Tune: BEACH SPRING, traditional American folk melody

SACRED PLACES - SATB

praise. Great the won - ders___ done a - mong___ us;___ daz - zling

deeds of truth___ and light. So, to - day in joy - ful

cho - rus we pro - claim Your pow'r and might.___

p cresc. e accel. poco a poco

26

28

sun - der;   sets your al - le - lu - ias   free.

Al - le - lu - ia! _____

THE POOL OF BETHESDA

Now there is in Jerusalem by the Sheep Gate a pool, which is called in Hebrew Bethesda, having five porticoes. In these lay a multitude of those who were sick, blind, lame, and withered, [waiting for the moving of the waters; for an angel of the Lord went down at certain seasons into the pool and stirred up the water; whoever then first, after the stirring up of the water, stepped in was made well from whatever disease with which he was afflicted.] A man was there who had been ill for thirty-eight years. When Jesus saw him lying there, and knew that he had already been a long time in that condition, He said to him, "Do you wish to get well?" The sick man answered Him, "Sir, I have no man to put me into the pool when the water is stirred up, but while I am coming, another steps down before me." Jesus said to him, "Get up, pick up your pallet and walk." Immediately the man became well, and picked up his pallet and began to walk.

John 5:2-12 (NASB)*

* Scripture taken from the NEW AMERICAN STANDARD BIBLE®, Copyright © 1960, 1962, 1963, 1968, 1971, 1972, 1973, 1975, 1977, 1995 by The Lockman Foundation. Used by permission.

MY SONG IN THE NIGHT

Words:
American Folk Hymn

Music by
JOSEPH M. MARTIN (BMI)
Incorporating tune:
EXPRESSION
American Folk Melody
The Sacred Harp, 1844

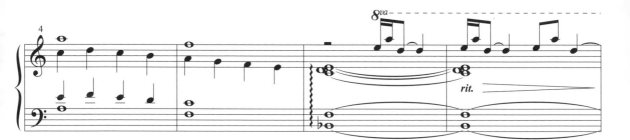

Copyright © 2016 by HAL LEONARD - MILWIN MUSIC CORP.
International Copyright Secured   All Rights Reserved

Duplication of this publication is illegal, and duplication is not granted
by the CCLI, LicenSing or OneLicense.net licenses.

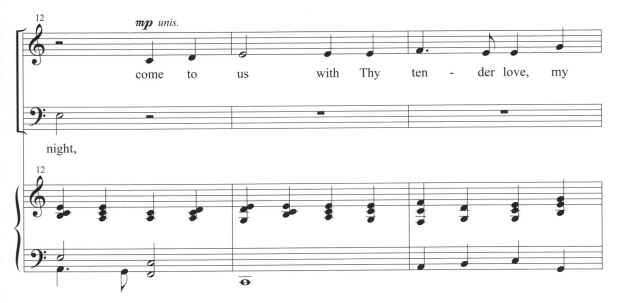

32

call; my_____ com - fort by day,_____ and my

song in the night.

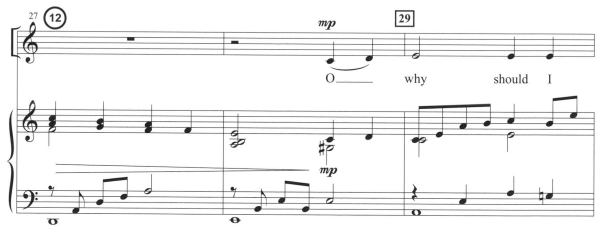

O_____ why should I

wan - der, a stran - ger from Thee;

light. ___ O ___ Je - sus, my Sav - ior, my ___

song in the night.

Je - sus, Je - sus, You are my

song._____ Je - sus, Je - sus,

You are my song in the night.

O_____

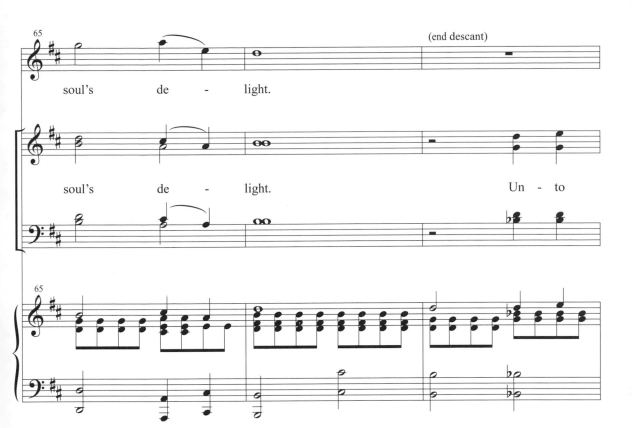

38

call; my com - fort by day, and my song in the

night. night, the night. O Je - sus, my Sav - ior, my night, the the night.
night.

night. song in the night, in the night.
night.

77 A little slower (♩ = ca. 88)

JERUSALEM

As they approached Jerusalem, Jesus sent two disciples, saying to them, "Go to the village ahead of you, and at once you will find a donkey tied there, with her colt by her. Untie them and bring them to Me. If anyone says anything to you, say that the Lord needs them, and he will send them right away."

This took place to fulfill what was spoken through the prophet:
"Say to the city of Zion,
'See, your King comes to you,
gentle and riding on a donkey,
and on a colt, the foal of a donkey.'"

The disciples went and did as Jesus had instructed them. They brought the donkey and the colt and placed their cloaks on them for Jesus to sit on. A very large crowd spread their cloaks on the road, while others cut branches from the trees and spread them on the road. The crowds that went ahead of Him and those that followed shouted,

"Hosanna to the Son of David!"
"Blessed is He who comes in the name of the Lord!"
"Hosanna in the highest heaven!"

When Jesus entered Jerusalem, the whole city was stirred and asked, "Who is this?"
The crowds answered, "This is Jesus, the prophet from Nazareth in Galilee."

Matthew 21:1-11 (adapted from NIV) *

* THE HOLY BIBLE, NEW INTERNATIONAL VERSION®, NIV® Copyright © 1973, 1978, 1984, 2011 by Biblica, Inc.® Used by permission. All rights reserved worldwide.

LIFT UP YOUR HEADS, JERUSALEM

Words and Music by
JOSEPH M. MARTIN (BMI)
Incorporating tunes:
PROMISED LAND
and **LAND OF REST**

* Tune: PROMISED LAND, American folk melody, *Southern Harmony*, 1835

Copyright © 2016 by HAL LEONARD - MILWIN MUSIC CORP.
International Copyright Secured   All Rights Reserved

**Duplication of this publication is illegal, and duplication is not granted
by the CCLI, LicenSing or OneLicense.net licenses.**

SACRED PLACES - SATB

* Words: Theodulph of Orleans, 760-821
  tr. John Mason Neale, 1818-1866

SACRED PLACES - SATB

42

honor to Thee, Redeemer, King; to

sana to the King;

whom the lips of children made sweet hosanas

ring. O blessed is He who

SACRED PLACES - SATB

44

high your glad ho - san - nas. Re - joice! Pre - pare the

way! Bless - ed is He who comes, who

comes in the name of the Lord. O bless - ed is the

48

THE UPPER ROOM

Then the day of Unleavened Bread came. That was the time the Passover lamb had to be sacrificed. Jesus sent Peter and John on ahead. "Go," He told them. "Prepare for us to eat the Passover meal."

"Where do you want us to prepare for it?" they asked.

Jesus replied, "When you enter the city, a man carrying a jar of water will meet you. Follow him to the house he enters. Then say to the owner of the house, 'The Teacher asks: Where is the guest room? Where can I eat the Passover meal with my disciples?' He will show you a large upstairs room with furniture already in it. Prepare for us to eat there."

Peter and John left. They found things just as Jesus had told them. So they prepared the Passover meal.

When the hour came, Jesus and His apostles took their places at the table. He said to them, "I have really looked forward to eating this Passover meal with you. I wanted to do this before I suffer. I tell you, I will not eat the Passover meal again until it is celebrated in God's kingdom."

Then Jesus took bread. He gave thanks and broke it. He handed it to them and said, "This is My body. It is given for you. Every time you eat it, do this in memory of Me."

In the same way, after the supper He took the cup. He said, "This cup is the new covenant in My blood. It is poured out for you."

Luke 22:7-16, 19-20 (adapted from NIRV) *

* NEW INTERNATIONAL READER'S VERSION® and NIrV® are registered trademarks of Biblica. Use of either trademark for the offering of goods or services requires the prior written consent of Biblica.

THE REMEMBERING

Words by
J. PAUL WILLIAMS (ASCAP)

American Folk Melody
Arranged by
JOSEPH M. MARTIN (BMI)

Copyright © 2009 by HAL LEONARD CORPORATION and HAL LEONARD - MILWIN MUSIC CORP.
This arrangement Copyright © 2016 by HAL LEONARD CORPORATION and HAL LEONARD - MILWIN MUSIC CORP.
International Copyright Secured   All Rights Reserved

Duplication of this publication is illegal, and duplication is not granted
by the CCLI, LicenSing or OneLicense.net licenses.

SACRED PLACES - SATB

52

54

SACRED PLACES - SATB

THE GARDEN OF GETHSEMANE

Then Jesus went with them to a place called Gethsemane, and He said to His disciples, "Sit here, while I go and pray." And taking with Him Peter and the two sons of Zebedee, He began to be sorrowful and troubled. Then He said to them, "My soul is very sorrowful, even to death; remain here, and watch with Me." And going a little farther He fell on His face and prayed, saying, "My Father, if it be possible, let this cup pass from Me; nevertheless, not as I will, but as You will."

*Matthew 26:36-39 (ESV)**

* The ESV® Bible (The Holy Bible, English Standard Version®).
Copyright © 2001 by Crossway, a publishing ministry of Good News Publishers.
The ESV® text has been reproduced in cooperation with and by permission of Good News Publishers.
Unauthorized reproduction of this publication is prohibited. All rights reserved.

THE MIDNIGHT GARDEN

Words by
JOSEPH M. MARTIN (BMI)

Tune: **SOJOURNER**
African-American Spiritual
Arranged by
JOSEPH M. MARTIN

* Tune: American folk melody, *Kentucky Harmony,* 1816

Copyright © 2016 by HAL LEONARD - MILWIN MUSIC CORP.
International Copyright Secured   All Rights Reserved

Duplication of this publication is illegal, and duplication is not granted
by the CCLI, LicenSing or OneLicense.net licenses.

SACRED PLACES - SATB

go _____ to the mid-night gar - den. _____ You must

go _____ to the hid - ing place. _____ In the

gar - den _____ there _ is _ mer - cy. _____ In _ the _

60

62

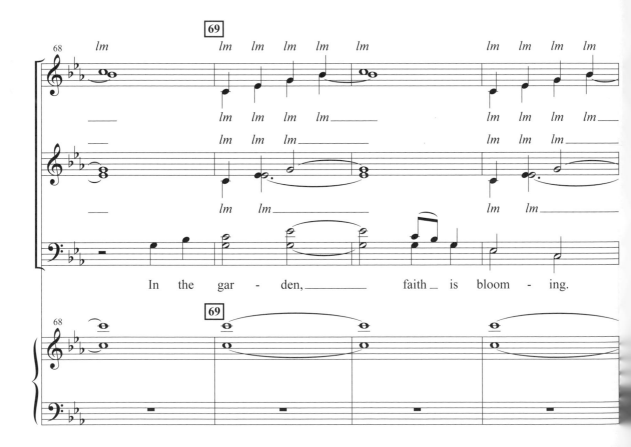

In ____ the __ shad-ows _____ God is near.

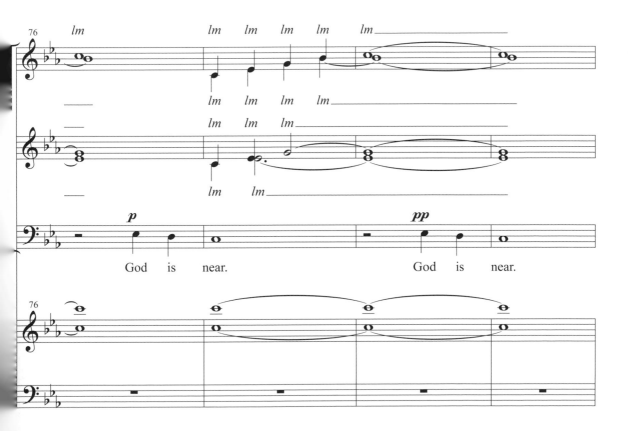

God is near. God is near.

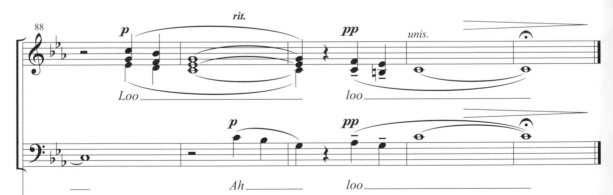

GOLGOTHA

And when they came to a place called Golgotha, which means Place of a Skull, they gave Him wine to drink mixed with gall; and after tasting it, He was unwilling to drink.

And when they had crucified Him, they divided up His garments among themselves by casting lots. And sitting down, they began to keep watch over Him there. And above His head they put up the charge against Him which read, "THIS IS JESUS THE KING OF THE JEWS."

Matthew 27:33-37 (NASB) *

* Scripture taken from the NEW AMERICAN STANDARD BIBLE®, Copyright © 1960, 1962, 1963, 1968, 1971, 1972, 1973, 1975, 1977, 1995 by The Lockman Foundation. Used by permission.

A GREEN HILL FAR AWAY

Words by
CECIL FRANCES ALEXANDER (1818-1895)

Tune: **CLEANSING FOUNTAIN**
American Folk Melody
Arranged by
JOSEPH M. MARTIN (BMI)

There _ is a green hill

Copyright © 2016 by HAL LEONARD - MILWIN MUSIC CORP.
International Copyright Secured   All Rights Reserved

Duplication of this publication is illegal, and duplication is not granted
by the CCLI, LicenSing or OneLicense.net licenses.

SACRED PLACES - SATB

far ____ a - way, with - out a cit - y ___ wall, where __

the dear Lord was cru - ci - fied, who __ died to save us

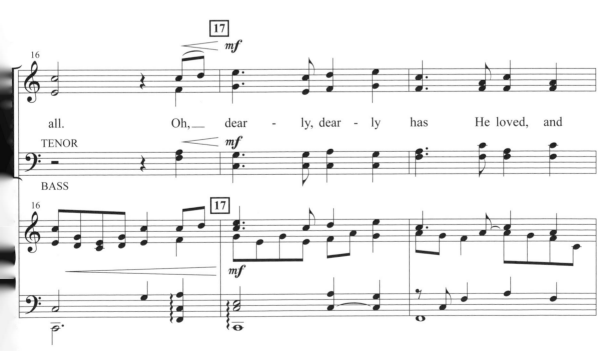

all. Oh, __ dear - ly, dear - ly has He loved, and

TENOR

BASS

SACRED PLACES - SATB

we ___ must love ___ Him ___ too; ___ and ___ trust ___ in His re-

deem - ing blood, and ___ try His works to do.

dim.

72

SACRED PLACES - SATB

74

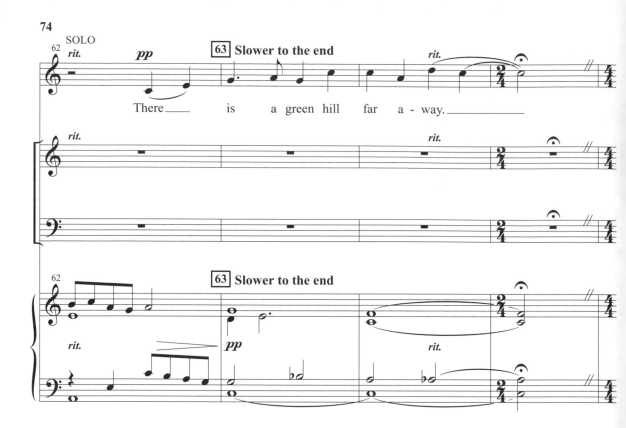

SUNRISE

Music by
JOSEPH M. MARTIN (BMI)

Freely, with expression (♩ = ca. 66)

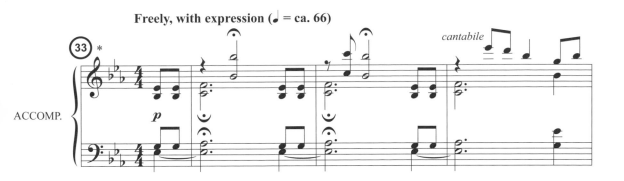

* Track 33 begins with 3 chimes prior to the first measure.

Copyright © 1993 by Malcolm Music, a div. of Shawnee Press, Inc.
This arrangement Copyright © 2016 by Malcolm Music, a div. of Shawnee Press, Inc.
International Copyright Secured   All Rights Reserved

Duplication of this publication is illegal, and duplication is not granted
by the CCLI, LicenSing or OneLicense.net licenses.

SACRED PLACES - SATB

THE GARDEN OF RESURRECTION

On the first day of the week, very early in the morning, the women took the spices they had prepared and went to the tomb. They found the stone rolled away from the tomb, but when they entered, they did not find the body of the Lord Jesus. While they were wondering about this, suddenly two men in clothes that gleamed like lightning stood beside them. In their fright the women bowed down with their faces to the ground, but the men said to them, "Why do you look for the living among the dead? He is not here; He has risen!"

Luke 24:1-6 (NIV)*

* THE HOLY BIBLE, NEW INTERNATIONAL VERSION®, NIV® Copyright © 1973, 1978, 1984, 2011 by Biblica, Inc.®
Used by permission. All rights reserved worldwide.

ALLELUIA! CHRIST IS RISEN!

Words and Music by
JOSEPH M. MARTIN (BMI)
Incorporating tunes:
HOLY MANNA
and **WARRENTON**

* Tune: HOLY MANNA, American folk melody, *Columbian Harmony*, 1825

Copyright © 2016 by HAL LEONARD - MILWIN MUSIC CORP.
International Copyright Secured   All Rights Reserved

Duplication of this publication is illegal, and duplication is not granted
by the CCLI, LicenSing or OneLicense.net licenses.

SACRED PLACES - SATB

* Optional shorter introduction.

SACRED PLACES - SATB

80

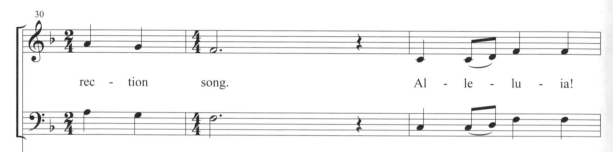

Now the morn - ing breaks with music.

All cre - a - tion finds its voice.

Dawn, at last, brings cel - e - bra - tion; fill - ing earth with

SACRED PLACES - SATB

Glo - ry be to God on high. Al - le - lu - ia!

Al - le - lu - ia! Lift your voic - es to the sky!

To the One who is wor - thy, let us

See God's glo - ry____ on dis - play.

See God's____ glo - ry on dis - play.

Now the gar - den blooms with____ prom - ise;

heav'n and earth in har - mo - ny.